Positive

Thinking

for

Life

"We are what we
repeatedly do.
Excellence, then,
is not an act, but a habit."

- Aristotle

Interactive reading

The Square Root Of Life is taking technology and innovation to the next level in interactive book publishing.

Throughout this book you will see scanable QR codes that will allow you to watch, listen, learn, visit and download information relevant to the topics within this book.

Interact and ENJOY!

All you need to do is use your tablet, iPhone, android smartphone or ipad QR scanner to scan the QR codes within the pages of this book to be redirected to the videos, opt-ins, downloads, audios and special offers. You can visit manually via your app store or Itunes store from your device to download a scanner.

Android QR Scanner App
:https://play.google.com/store/apps/details?id=me.scan.android.client
IPhone & Ipad QR Scanner App:
https://itunes.apple.com/en/app/qr-reader-for-iphone/id368494609?mt=8

If you do not have an android device, iPhone or ipad to scan the QR codes, simply view videos and audio from Sarah at:

www.squarerootoflife.com.au

Fundamental techniques for

Positive Thinking:

Learn to remove stress,

beat depression

and start living

the life

YOU WANT TODAY!

First Edition 2014
Copyright © 2014 by Sarah Davis.
All rights reserved. No part of this publication may be reproduced, stored in a retrieval system, or transmitted in any form or by any means, electronic, mechanical, photocopying, recording or otherwise, without the prior written permission from publisher: SQRoL Publications

National Library of Australia
Cataloguing-in-Publication entry:
Sarah Jayne Davis 1976

Title: Positive thinking for life / Sarah Davis.
ISBN: 9780992416508 (paperback)
Series: Davis, Sarah J., Square root of life.
Subjects: Self-actualization (Psychology)
Conduct of life.

Dewey Number: 158.1

ISBN: 0992416507 (pbk)
ISBN-13: 978-0-9924165-0-8 (pbk.)
Self Published Edition / SQRoL Publications
Email. tosarahdavis@gmail.com
                    For Further information about orders: Phone: +61 422648079

√Life

THE SQUARE ROOT OF LIFE

It only takes one

One cell to create a living thing

One dream to create a life

One hope to return life from hopelessness

One person to save a life

One tree to sprout a thousand vines

One thought to become a reality

One book to change your thoughts

One idea to change your mindset

If you had to come up with the number of total life experiences you have encountered until today, it would be the tens of thousands. We lead a complex existence that has endless experiences. These seemingly unrelated experiences make up who we are today, they define how we think, how we respond and react to the world around us.

The square root of life = YOU

Dedication

This book is dedicated to my son Ayrton

For giving me purpose and for being my "why".

To the readers:

We are all alike; choosing to evolve and learning to better ourselves.

This book contains "life tools"

To help you fulfil your goals, live a better life.

and

Be the best you!

"The cave you fear to enter

holds the treasure

you seek"

- Joseph Campbell

Forward Michael Kirton

Sarah Davis has written these books from a personal place of complete conviction as to the effectiveness of their capacity to change lives. Since I have known her she has moved from personal circumstances which were difficult and negative to a wonderful and enlightened view of life. Now living that way, she reflects the enthusiasm which she has incorporated into her words and work.

She has a tremendous energy for her life at present which has come from her own application to the principles she espouses in her books. The reason they are alive and workable is that they were all part of the program she set herself in her own efforts to changing her mind, body and emotions using the practical and spiritual tools she covers in order to achieve her own goals.

It was a great surprise and very exciting to me to first read her material and see where she had come in her pathway of vigorous and enlightened reflection and application to finding the meaning and source of life and living in this Age. I hope that her readers find her inspiration and use some of her insight to help themselves in stamping their own imprint on the blueprint of the life energy we all share.

I am sure that readers who follow this pathway will find their own strengths and personal meaning in themselves as has Sarah.

Michael

Contents

Introduction

The purpose of this book is to explain that although we all have inner conflict which prevents us from enjoying the life we deserve – we can triumph over it.

Living with abundance and happiness is a mindset that successful people seem to have mastered. Learning the easy techniques in this book and by having the intention to change your life, you can do just that. Strong intent is required to live a better life without exception.

Understand simple daily processes can be adapted into your life which will ultimately redesign your future. You will be learning to enhance your thoughts, dictate your paradigms and create enlightenment within.

Various books have been written on the Law of Attraction, which is the name given to the belief that "like attracts like" and that by focusing on positive or negative thoughts, one can bring about positive or negative results. Most books about the Law of Attraction give you the tools required to use this law, they do not detail techniques required to take immediate ACTION, so you can apply the LAW and adapt it into your life.

I have gained phenomenal knowledge of the Law of Attraction and its power, and with this knowledge I have compiled the "The Square Root of Life" manuals or "life" work books, if you like, so that you can learn how to apply these fantastic tools.

With this book you will learn the process on both a conscious and subconscious level, through your own written work and mental awareness.

These books require you to participate, practise and develop the skills in each chapter, you'll find "notes" pages available at the back of this publication.

Your **BONUS FREE OFFER** ; in this print edition – is the Square Root of Life workbook – FREE for you to download & print out as many times as you need simply go to: & Print it off !

www.squarerootoflife.com.au/bonus

Re-reading & re-doing the tasks in this manual will continue to refresh your perception, continually freeing yourself each time you use it.

The difference between one another is simply experiences. Change is tough, if you are like most people it will be an uphill battle that requires persistence and endurance continually facing self sabotage or self defeating behaviour at every step.

Through these tasks you will firstly identify what is affecting your mental process, by identifying the issues you subconsciously battle each day will help your chain of thought change direction. Redefining your paradigms regarding the issues you face and what you truly believe about yourself and others. Once you work toward eliminating any of the issues that are affecting your life in the present, you can begin to work on your thought processes.

Negative thoughts are found to have to largest overall affect on your emotional persona. Eliminating those thoughts will be the second process you follow in this book. Changing your immediate thought patterns and instilling upward thinking is something that everyone should develop. Then controlling the mind and its reaction is the third set of skills to develop.

Meditating and relaxing is crucial for the overall amount of change and success you will encounter. The forth process you will learn in this book is how to meditate on a habitual scale. Hopefully you will find meditation easier to adapt into everyday life.

Setting goals and creating drive for your desires, ignites passion from within your deepest crevices', this will be the fifth part of the process and finally affirming what you are becoming and what path you decide to follow.

I have tried to avoid intricate explanations, I find too many books filled with verbal fodder that really distracts from the main point being explained. I have attempted to keep the text in a "workbook mode", creating a simple understanding of the tasks at hand.

This book has a lot of techniques that require you to participate; there are also links to audio and video at;

www.squarerootoflife.com.au/techniques

Chapter 1

Paradigms

"Your paradigm is so intrinsic to your mental process that you are hardly aware of its existence,

until you try to communicate

with someone with a different paradigm"

Donella Meadows

Ruling Mental State

Your mental state completely defines you and your outer experiences!

Being able to change your mental state is an uncommon skill, and must be learnt, applied and mindfully mastered. It is a powerful ability that enables you to live more effectively, positively and in harmonious, effortless flow,

We must be conscious of what we are feeling and thinking, as our inner state controls how we function. Have you ever been in a bad mood that has escalated to a severe alienation of everything around you? And you were unable to shake the mood at all.

Your whole mental setup is related to how you feel and what you are thinking at any given moment. The reason that our life spirals out of control in the face of turmoil, is due to a constant negative thought and bad feelings, which in turn dictates what mood we will be in, and is in fact actually *creating* our experiences, setting us up for more bad things.

You need to be aware of what you are thinking about and feeling. The first few chapters of this book are related to getting the right mental state, focusing on what inspires us and making a choice about what we allow to enter our minds.

Our body is a great tool for creating emotions, along with the mind. Have you ever noticed that when you are feeling down, your body language says it too? Drooping shoulders, scowling, feet dragging along the floor are all outward signs of a negative emotional state. Use your body to help you change your state of mind. Shoulders back, chest puffed up, stand tall, smile on your dial, swing in your step: all these bodily actions help get your mental state to its prime conditioning.

Revaluate your life...   Who are you?

Do you like who you have become?

Your paradigm dictates your logic.

Working with your subconscious mind will change your paradigm and your programming.   We have three parts to our complete being:

1   Our spiritual being
2   Our intellect
3   Our physical body

Your inner belief dictates your paradigm, so changing your inner beliefs can change your paradigms and consequently your life; on all levels of your being. We need to set our inner beliefs and unlearn what we have been programmed by our upbringing and from society. Change what you have been raised to believe....

We must understand what we "really" believe and know which beliefs to change.

Setting new paradigms or new ways of thinking is imperative to becoming a better person and developing our inner spirit. By analysing what we currently perceive, we can change our paradigms and ultimately change our lives.

What is a paradigm?   Example:

Some people believe that they are lucky and they seem to always win. On another paradigm if someone's belief is that "Oh I never win anything" indicatively they never do and are likely never too win!

Some people believe "I am fat"; they can never seem to lose weight, – others may have inner thoughts telling them "I am happy with my body" "I look great in this" and they *do*!

Whether you say it or it is your inner thought – that is what happens in your reality.

You must:

Undo your past way of thinking and ingrain a new belief system to conquer any achievement followed by action. You simply can't believe that you never get sick and eat fast food, for you will lack nutrition and suffer the adverse health consequences.

Your actions must also match your beliefs. But first we need to consider what aspect of life we would like to change and from where the belief system stems from. Don't fall into the trap of thinking or wishing for change without acting.

- What is affecting your life at the moment?
- What areas most require immediate change?

Maybe you are unhappy with your partner, in your workplace, with your children's behavior or your own daily thought process.

What do you believe is stopping you from living with happiness and love in all areas of your life?

Task: *(Chapter 2 – In your workbook)*

Please take your workbook and write down:
Areas needing change – problems you feel you are currently facing

List them on the page, leaving a big gap around each word
Every new word- approximately a 3 line space / gap

Write down every ailment that you feel you are experiencing
Everything that is affecting your happiness or causing sadness

If you need to, do this over a few pages feel free to continually write down each issue that is affecting your happiness in day to day life and leave a gap between every issue.

Your list may look something like the following;

Marriage	Relationship
Income	Feel too stressed
Family relationships	Childs getting naughtier
Friendships	Having better friends
Stress	Depressed
Wealth	Managing money
Health	Getting fit

Brainstorming and mind mapping

ow we are going to do a brainstorm for each of these words.

Draw a mind map for each word; mind mapping looks generally something like this:

For every word that you have written on your page circle the word then draw lines outwardly from it and write what you believe are the issues on this topic, what are the problems you face?

If you have written marriage; what in the marriage?

You will probably end up with something like this:

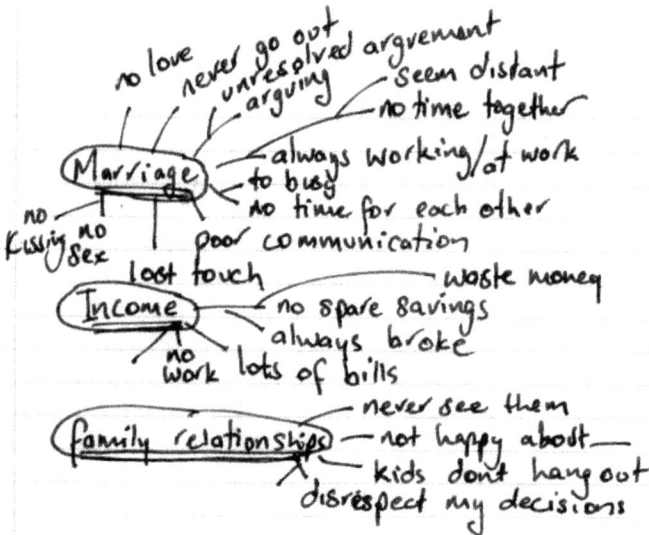

You need to recognise areas where you feel problems. Only "you" know the cause and effect these are having on your life, so only you are able to source them.

In the first topic of this example, "marriage," we can identify that there are a few issues we are not happy about – these issues have only come about due to our beliefs and on what is happening within our "marriage".
The paradigm we have about marriage allows us to feel worse about the current situation than needed. If you believe that marriage was supposed to be a period of nonstop bliss, yet all that you currently endure is pain and suffering, then your thought process has to change and to accept that marriage needs work in the areas you have noted.

Task: (Chapter 2 – In your workbook)

Turn the page of your note book-
Re-write the list > same words

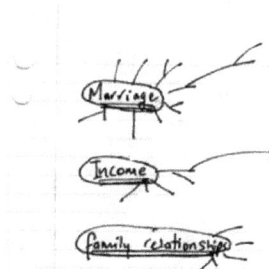

Draw another mind mapping diagram with the same word in the circle, only this time, write the opposite to the original mind mapping "arm" you have on page 1.

Write each arm again outlining "How" you can correct or solve the issue on page 1. Describe the reverse or opposite.

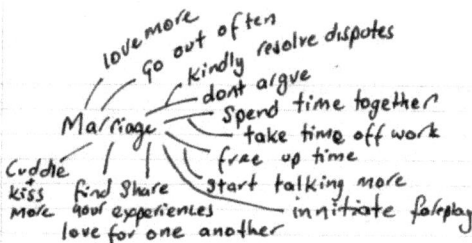

By doing this task you will identify exactly how to "*self*-correct" the problems that you feel you are facing.

Action is always required to move forward and resolve problems. *You* hold the power to correct and change the process for the future- once you have identified how issues can be reversed logically, it eliminates a part of your subconscious that keep telling you what is wrong and then you can move forward knowing that you are intentionally working towards fixing the problems.

It works because that our intellect understands reversing the areas, showing our spiritual level simple opposites, so that we can then work on a physical level to change these issues.
The inner belief will then become "I am working toward a great marriage" by thinking how to correct it, rather than to believe "I have so many problems with my marriage". You are now shifting your paradigm (belief), and taking responsibility to change your current circumstance with any issue you are facing.

It is a simple mind game that can easily reverse how you approach issues, how you think about what is currently happening and taking control to correct what you are not happy about.

Spend as much time as you can on all the issues that you believe you are struggling with right now.

Task: *(Chapter 3 – In your workbook)*

Write each issue down, brainstorm your issues and mind map the subject, and then reverse your issues.
This will simply identify a way to logically correct issues surrounding you that may be affecting your happiness, which is creating a paradigm and attracting the opposite of what you really want.

Make a list of each statement.
Using the second page, make a list explaining how you will correct the issue.

For example:
Marriage; I will organise to go out more often,
I will try to show more love,
I will resolve our disputes kindly,
I will make sure we spend more time together, etc.– list each reversal.

Then under each mind map issue; write your new paradigm / belief to the issue

i.e.;
Marriage; I will work on having the best marriage,
Income: I am in control of managing my money better,
Stress: I am working towards relieving all of my stress and living a happier life

Creating your "Cue"

Once you have eliminated the immediate worry by shifting your paradigm and affirming within your subconscious that you are working on bettering each situation, you can now find your "cue".

Your "cue" is a thought imagery that you will repeatedly think of to change your mindset. It helps you redirect your focus to an exhilarating, purely positive vision or scenario, so you bounce back from frustration or negative feelings into your "cue" vibe.

Follow the following guidelines for creating your cue:

> ➢ It needs to be something that helps resonate pure happiness and exhilaration
> ➢ Something or sometime that immediately changes how you feel
> ➢ It must snap you back into a positive thought
> ➢ It's a visual, mental and physical imagery that converts your thought process
> ➢ The cue needs to transform your thinking to immediate positive thought

You will be creating your cue to signal thought change. When negative thoughts surface, using your cue, take five seconds to prompt a new emotion will inevitably change your thought process from negative to positive.

Task: (Chapter 4 – In your workbook)

One a new page, write down all of the wonderful events that have happened in your life,

i.e.: birth of your child, your wedding day, buying your 1ˢᵗ car, proposing to your wife, etc

Make a list and take 5 seconds for each event and close your eyes and find out which one brings you immediate joy and has the most overwhelming excitement and gratitude.

This is your "CUE" > remember this event as a mental savior!

Why is your "cue" important?

Having a "cue" is creating a trigger that allows you to take control of your mental processing. This is also known as cognitive shifting. A "cue" is a mood repair strategy that shifts a person's mood from negative and general sadness or clinical depression to a greater contentment or happiness.

Shifting your mental processing as it happens is also known as cognitive shifting.

Wikipedia explains:

Cognitive shifting is a method used in awareness management describing the mental process of re-directing one's focus of attention away from one fixation and toward a different focus of attention. This shifting process can be initiated either by habit and unconsciously, or as an act of conscious volition.

In the general framework of cognitive therapy and awareness management, cognitive shifting refers to the conscious choice to take charge of one's mental habits—and redirect one's focus of attention in helpful, more successful directions. In the term's specific usage in corporate awareness methodology, cognitive shifting is a performance-oriented technique for refocusing attention in more alert, innovative, charismatic and empathic directions

Mood repair strategies
Most of the techniques listed in this book, are Mood repair strategies, using them to avoid negative moods or in pursuit of positive moods. Each strategy has different results with different individuals. Learn which techniques help you take control and live a happier existence, different personality types may be more receptive to some tasks than others.

Using as many as you can, observe which work better for you and incorporating them into your routine will primarily distract you from current mood swings and overall uplift your positivity.

"Always aim at complete harmony of thought
and word and deed.
Always aim at purifying
your thoughts and everything
will be well."
Mahatma Gandhi

Chapter 2

Mind

Control

"The mind is everything,
what you think
you become"

Buddha

Snce you have **mind control,**

your life will change.

Michael W. Kirton, a clinical psychologist taught me many of these techniques. {**Clinical psychology** is an integration of science, theory and clinical knowledge for the purpose of understanding, preventing, and relieving psychologically-based distress or dysfunction and to promote subjective well-being and personal development. >Wikipedia}

Mind control is not something that you can acquire easily, but with enough daily repetition, practice and an inner willingness to apply these tasks, you will be able to instill a habit that corrects what your mind thinks and how you feel.

When you realise your mind is wandering off track or dwelling on people or events that have affected you emotionally, you can correct the pattern of thought by bringing it back to a place of peace and normality.

It is very normal for each of us to experience thousands of thoughts even when we don't realise that they are happening. Many times we dwell on hardship or negativity that can alter our mood and send us into deep depression; these thoughts can be consciously and also subconsciously.

It is normal to have conflicting thoughts and feelings about any subject. Our inner conflict is like a private war within, creating scattered or unpredictable behavior and thoughts leading to depression, self-sabotage and internal stress.

Knowing that we all suffer from these inner conflicts is usually quite liberating. It's not just you, everyone experiences that kind of "emotional tug of war", but being able to identify and resolve these conflicts can be challenging.

The following world-renowned techniques are taught by many professional psychologists. They are shared with people mostly suffering depression or anxiety, in order to assist them.

Following them correctly will take time and you will need to practice them a few times to be able to get the full effect and to be able to use them when needed.

The "Reset" technique

a. Take time out when you are struggling with a negative emotions or thoughts
b. Sit up straight, relax your mind, breathe slowly and deeply
c. Circular breathing: in through your nose and out through your mouth
d. Concentrate on your stomach region and feel each breathe coming past your organs: lungs, heart, stomach and out through your solar plexus.
e. Slowly breathe in and out, holding the breath for a moment before breathing out
f. Do this breathing technique about 8 times

Recall the issue you are getting upset or agitated about; past or present

Recall how it felt and what you were feeling

a. Keep breathing past your lungs and through your heart to your stomach and exhale – an additional 8 times

Now recall a time in your life when you were really happy

RESET your emotion: Feel <u>that</u> emotion, imagine the genuine love for that moment

FEEL this throughout your body

a. Now ask your heart; "How can I manage this better"
b. Listen to the 1st thought that comes into your head
c. Then say;

"Thank you heart"

NB; Key elements to this are to "shift" attention to the area of the heart and stomach region whilst, you "activate" a positive feeling and then "sense" what the best attitude for the affecting situation is; Reset your emotion through thought and feeling

Task:
Initially you should practise doing this around 8 times per day as needed, when you are struggling with a lot of negative emotions, stop and breathe and "reset" your emotions, this will relieve immediate stress and redirect your chain of thought.

Asking your heart is the inner spirit. What is best solution to the problem? The automatic response is what you need to listen too.

You can scan and follow the audio instructions

Audio techniques;

Once you replace negative thoughts with positive ones, you'll start having positive results.

Willie Nelson

Mindfulness

Our thoughts often produce negative emotions. You need to change your thoughts and "make good."

    a. Take time out, sit up, relax and breathe deeply

    b. Circular breathing: in through your nose and out through your mouth

    c. Concentrate on your heart region and feel each breathe coming through your heart and out through your solar plexus.

    d. Slowly breathe in and out, holding the breath for a moment before breathing out

    e. Close your eyes

Be aware of the negative or bad thought

Watch your thought, see your thought, without giving it emotion

Hold the thought out at arm's length: see the thought in your hand - have no emotion it – just view it in your hand – it does not affect you, as you watch the thought either;

    a. Watch it fade away until it disappears to nothing

    b. Brush them away with a feather, till they slowly disappear

Affirm your strengths – tell yourself;

    a. This is not what I think

    b. My thought does not control me

    c. I control what I'm thinking

Continue deep breathing throughout the exercise – practice when things are going well!

Task: This should be practised daily, whenever you are getting negative thoughts, have a little time to perform a "reset", this will relieve immediate stress.

Heart activate

    a.   Take time out, sit up, relax and breathe deeply

    b.   Circular breathing: in through your nose and out through your mouth

    c.   Concentrate on your heart region and feel each breath coming through your heart and out through your solar plexus.

    d.   Slowly breathe in and out, holding the breath for a moment before breathing out

    e.   Do this breathing technique about 8 times

Activate a genuine feeling of appreciation or care for someone or something in your life use your "cue" and make a sincere effort to sustain a positive feeling of appreciation or care

Dwell upon this feeling of gratitude or love throughout your being

If your mind starts wandering, gently focus your breathing back through the heart and solar plexus and reconnect with feelings of care or appreciation.

After you're finished, sincerely sustain your feelings as long as you can.

NB; this technique is a simple way to cultivate and amplify positive feelings. You will gain a sense of inner warmth, feelings of harmony and it will have nourishing effects on your mind and body.

Task: This should be used when you are getting negative thoughts and have only a brief moment to collect your thoughts use this to relieve immediate stress in less time.

Love and Kindness

    a.   Take time out, sit up, relax and breathe deeply
    b.   Circular breathing: in through your nose and out through your mouth
    c.   Concentrate on your heart region and feel each breathe coming through your heart and out through your solar plexus.
    d.   Slowly breathe in and out, holding the breath for a moment before breathing out
    e.   Close your eyes

Imagine a radiant bright light coming down through your centre, from the centre of your head through your chest and heart.

See the luminous bright white light spreading through your entire body. Feel the warmth as tension begins to release from your shoulders, back through to your legs and feet.

Take 8 even, slow, deep breaths, as you imagine your whole being consumed in the brightness.

As you inhale, feel more light is being absorbed into your body, filling your body and touching your outer parts like your eyes and throat, hands and feet.

As you exhale, feels darkness leave your inner self as the light within you shines brighter and clearer.

Softly say, "I radiate light, I am powerful energy, I have the power to heal myself and all those around me, with inner brightness I attract love and positive energy, I have compassion for all"

If your mind starts wandering, gently focus your breathing back through the heart and solar plexus and reconnect with feelings of care or appreciation.

Then, sit quietly for several minutes. Open your eyes.

Conscious thought

a. Take time out, sit up, relax and breathe deeply
b. Circular breathing: in through your nose and out through your mouth
c. Concentrate on your heart region and feel each breathe coming through your heart and out through your solar plexus.
d. Slowly breathe in and out, holding the breath for a moment before breathing out
e. Close your eyes

Concentrate on the moment and whatever is present in that moment.

Feel your stomach and chest rise and fall with each breath.

Once settled and relaxed, widen your awareness to include all the sensations in your body as well as any thoughts or feelings. Imagine yourself in an open field, see the clouds and blue sky, feel the sunshine touching your skin.

If you find yourself swept up in thought or emotion, notice it and simply return to the circular breathing. Imagine yourself in the field and notice all around you: trees, grass, birds....

Pay attention to the ever-changing process of thinking rather than to the contents of your thoughts.
As you begin to see that they are indeed just thoughts, they will begin to lose their power. You will no longer believe everything you think!

Continue to watch and become mindful of your thoughts, feelings, and sensations for around 10 - 20 minutes.

Language

Negative words can significantly affect your brain, even more so over the long term.

If you vocalise your negativity, or even slightly frown when you say "no," more stress chemicals will be released, not only in your brain, but in the listener's brain as well. (Psychology today.com) So even using the word "no" stress signals are passed through the brain and are disrupting your brain function in a negative way.

Foul language has a huge negative effect, even when uttered without emotion and with no desire to offend, like swearing when telling a joke, foul language triggers strong emotional responses of the brain, causing the brain to partially shut down and go into a defensive mode known as the "fight or flight" response. Swearing actually stresses the brain on a deep cognitive level as do negative thoughts.

Constant use of swearing or negative thoughts can cause the brain to stay in a defensive mode, in turn producing stress-induced analgesia. These reactions to swearing are automatic neurological responses that we have no control over and can produce feelings of depression.
Even though swearing may be a very impulsive behavior and although the words may release immediate frustration or anger, you are actually causing a deep emotional reaction with notable neurological consequences.
So for heaven's sake and your own ... don't swear! ☺

When you are positive and say positive words rather than negative ones, you will feel much better. Remember that words can change your brain.

1   Do not vocalise negative rumination, which stimulates release of destructive neurochemicals related to "fight or flight"

2   Do not speak in anger or act irrationally – that does even more damage

3   Ask "is this situation *really* a threat to my survival?"

4   Interrupt the amygdala's reaction to an imagined threat, take action and resolve

5   Reframe your mind by focusing on positive words or images

6   Must repetitiously and consciously generate positive thoughts at a 5:1 ratio (positive versus negative)

7   Words and thoughts propel the motivational centres of the brain into action

8   Choose your words wisely and speak them slowly

9   5 : 1 (5 positive thoughts to every 1 negative thought) generates optimal brain range functioning to engage positive thinking – so for every negative thought immediately think of 5 positive thoughts to eliminate neurological responses to the negative thought... that is the power of YES

Also to reduce your stress level and increases brain development, try listening to Mozart (it might sound lame but hunt through his work and find a song that you like), or pop music such as Blur's "Country House," "Return of the Mack," by Mark Morrison and PJ and Duncan's "Stepping Stone." Research also shows that they also improved the brain's cognitive function.

In short, don't swear. Listen to some relaxing tunes and enhance your mind. ☺

Task: *(Chapter 5 – In your workbook)*

Take a moment to Google some of the above songs and listen to them.

Write down all of the songs above in your journal, to remind you later on which songs have proven "brain stimulating" reactions

Download them to your play list or purchase them on a CD
Try to take the time to listen to one each day!

Every day we have plenty of opportunities
to get angry, stressed or offended.
But what you're doing when you indulge
these negative emotions is giving
something outside yourself
power over your happiness.
You can choose to not let
little things upset you.

Joel Osteen

Chapter 3

Master Thought Process

"Change your thoughts and
you change your world"

Norman Vincent Peale

Master Process

*R*udolf Steiner (an early 20th century philosopher) proposed six simple exercises to develop and purify thinking, feeling and willing, called *"the six basic exercises."*

Thinking, feeling and willing are parts of the soul. By practicing them - first separately (thinking, feeling, willing) and then in combinations - you develop your soul.

Sometimes you may find that thinking, feeling and willing, happen automatically and that some thoughts, feelings and actions are not so pretty. By doing the basic exercises, you can purify them.

The aim of the exercises
- To be more aware of how you think, feel and act.
- To gain more control over thoughts, feelings and actions.
- To think, feel and act more clearly.
- To make a harmonious whole of thinking, feeling and willing.

Do these exercises every day consecutively for around 4 weeks. This will enable you to create thought habits and acquire necessary skills. You can do them alone or in a group which will encourage the participants and encourage longer sessions. They may become a more tedious after the first or second week, and the novelty will wear off, to generate more enthusiasm and remember your "why": "why" you decided to start self-improvement initially.

You can listen to the techniques here;

> *"As a single footstep will not make a path on the earth, so a single thought will not make a pathway in the mind. To make a deep physical path, we walk again and again. To make a deep mental path, we must think over and over the kind of thoughts we wish to dominate our lives"* Henry David Thoreau

The six basic exercises

1. Control of thought

Use an ordinary object (a pencil, key, etc.) and think about it for five minutes every day. Take an object in-front of you or in your mind and the first time you describe it to yourself aloud. You can also imagine yourself describing it to a blind person.
Use all your senses and make as many observations as you can in five minutes. Repeat this the next day; you will probably notice new details.

After a while you can ask questions about the object: "What can I do with it?",

"What is it made of?", "Why this shape?", "What other shapes could it have?", "Where was it made?", "How did I get it?"," How are the raw materials mined?", etc.
You will be able to answer some of these questions. If not, you can search for an answer in an encyclopedia or on the internet. You should be able to determine whether your thoughts are correct; otherwise, your thoughts will wander.

You can repeat what you did the day before and build on your previous thoughts. After some time you will have covered all possible questions, then do it one or two more times until you can really find no more issues to think about. Then follow the same procedure with another object. When doing this exercise you may notice that your thinking gets clearer and sharper, and that your perception, concentration and objectivity increase. Also, your interest grows.

The difficulty of the exercise is that your mind wanders. The challenge is to be able to think about the object for five minutes. Another difficulty may be that you do not have the answers to the questions. However, nowadays it is easy to find them on the internet.

The exercise is called *control of the mind*. The example just given shows that often there is no control over our thinking. We are thought, and our thinking is associative and automatic. We believe that we think, but our thinking is often not focused.

Make sure that you do the exercise every day, preferably at a fixed time, when you are awake and clear-headed; for example, not after dinner, but before or after breakfast or at 8 o'clock at night. You can also do it while waiting for the train, in a spare moment.
Doing the exercise with two or three objects should be sufficient.

2. Control of will

Do a simple act without purpose at a fixed time each day.
You decide to do a simple act daily at a fixed time during a period of four weeks. The exercise is called *acting on your own initiative*. This act does not have a meaning until itself and is only useful as an exercise. The act could be anything: pulling your left earlobe, untying and tying your shoelaces, rolling back one sleeve of your sweater. The variations are endless, but make sure that you have the necessary attribute with you when you need it.

If you can, do the exercise at the same fixed time every day. The challenge is not in the act itself but in adhering to a fixed, structured schedule for it. If you are late for the exercise, it is still good to do it. The fixed time means that you must keep your aim and at the same time restrain yourself until the time has come. Your awareness of what you really want will grow as a result. The goal is to take the initiative in your actions, to better direct your will and to remain steadfast.

Many actions over the course of a day are performed because they have to be done or they are carried out for other people. There are few acts that we really do for ourselves. The exercise is a commitment to yourself to do something. Such a commitment is harder to keep than a commitment to someone else.

Some tips to make this exercise a success:

· It helps to choose a time that is easy. If you wake up every day at seven, you can do it shortly thereafter. Often you will see that when you are in a different rhythm, the exercise is more difficult to do. You will succeed during the week, for instance, but not so easily in the weekends. On those days you will have to make more of an effort.

· Imagine a picture in the morning of performing the act at the place and in the circumstances where you expect to be at the fixed time. If you hold on to that image, it is more likely that your exercise will succeed.

· If you do the exercise lightly, using your sense of humour, it is easier to maintain and will make you even happier when the exercise succeeds.

· If it is very difficult to do the exercise, then put a note on the wall to remind you.

3.   Equanimity

- the exercise of feeling

Observe your feelings, restrain strong responses and strengthen feeble ones.

This exercise is not done with an object or at a fixed time, but throughout the day.

When something happens to you, look at your feelings, either at that moment or later. At first you might not experience many different feelings, but in the course of four weeks there appear to be more and more, both positive and negative, both fierce and feeble reactions. It may help to make a list or a map of your feelings and their intensity at the end of the day.

Feelings are like the weather. They are just there. We experience them, but unlike the weather we can adjust our reaction by our thoughts. An example: I say something to someone. He leaves the room and the door closes with a bang. I get scared and feel fear. Is this banging of the door a response to what I said? Did I hurt him? But is this thought justified? Perhaps the door was shut by a gust of wind. When the person comes back and smiles or says something like "my grip on the doorknob slipped," then I am reassured and understand that my response was not correct and slowly I will be able to change my attitude to the slamming of a door. Next time I will be less scared and perhaps I am more neutral to such an event. Another example: when I am pushed in my back while walking in the street, I feel anger, annoyance or fear. When I see that I was pushed by a blind person, I understand that he could not help it.

Perhaps thought leads to a modified feeling about the event. And I can take it a step further by cultivating the thought: "Others may be blind to how they affect others. It is their ignorance or failure to see, that leads others to act towards me

- 39 -

in ways that may evoke my anger." Then, gradually, this thought permeates us and our feelings and reactions become modified.

Maybe they are not as intense, or they don't last so long anymore. You cannot take a particular moment, but you need to restrain your strong responses at the moment that you experience them, and likewise cherish the subtle ones.

When you look back at the end of the day, you will find that sometimes you could do that, and that you missed an opportunity at other times. The next day you go on with that awareness.

Real feelings usually start with "I am", e.g. angry, happy, sad, surprised. It can help to make a list of feelings.

This list is from the Centre for Nonviolent Communication.

Goal of Equanimity

• To become aware of the feelings you have and their intensity. *Observe* your feelings. Make an inventory of them and their intensity once or several times a day or at the end of the day.

You use your feeling as an instrument of perception because it tells you about your relationship with your surroundings and yourself. You will notice that there are feelings that you often have. You will also notice that some feelings are intense and that there are feelings that are less developed, hard to perceive and rarely or not expressed.

• To be aware how your thoughts influence your feelings. The closer you can stick to your observations, the less your feelings will overwhelm you.

• To create harmony and balance in your feelings. Control and weaken violent reactions and strengthen subtle and weak emotions, thus assuring emotional equilibrium.

The aim is not to deny feelings but to diminish the violent reaction, so that other more subtle emotions can be felt. It is then that you take charge of your feelings and not vice versa. You should not suppress the anger per se, but the involuntary cursing.

Result of Equanimity

"You are not your feelings, you have them." You become more receptive to feelings and can experience them more evenly. Balance, awareness, and equanimity arise.

You are able to identify your feelings, they belong to you, are part of you. By observing them, you create a certain distance to your feelings. They can no longer sweep you away. You control yourself and your feelings better. You are able to keep your composure.

4. **Positivity**

Always try to see the positive aspects of something negative.

In many situations, you see the negative and ugly aspects quite clearly. In this exercise the aim is that you always see something positive, too, without denying the negative.

The exercise should not lead to an uncritical attitude and a vague "everything is good and beautiful" or to denying the negative. But there is always something beautiful or good that lies concealed in everything.

The exercise is built on the previous exercises; it is a new step because of the combination of thinking and feeling. To see the positive in the negative, you have to overcome your reactions, opinions and prejudices. Questions like "What does this tell me?", "What can I learn from this?", "Why is it that I did not hear?" may help in this exercise.

A good opportunity to practice this are reviews, evaluations, etc.: you always mention one more positive point then a negative one.

There are two aspects to this exercise:

· Strengthening the perception. You must not let the negative or the ugly distract you from looking for the positive. You strengthen your interest by searching for that.

· Becoming independent of your feelings by looking for the positive. You have to restrain your negative feelings; otherwise they keep you away from further observation.

During and after this exercise you still see the negative, but you try to find something positive in it. Sometimes this only succeeds when you look back, which may be days or even years later. As you observe more and see the situation from different angles, you will restrain your opinion at first and you become more open and will observe more comprehensively. Therefore the exercise leads to greater tolerance. Ultimately, there is almost nothing that does not have something positive in it.

5. Open-mindedness
be open to new experiences

Always keep open the possibility to experience something new and keep in mind that new experiences can counter old ones.

For the umpteenth time you stroll through the woods, everything is already known. Suddenly, you notice that the light falls through the leaves or the high grass of a meadow in a special way or that the colours are different and of a special intensity. You suddenly smell an unknown fragrance.

The fact that you notice this makes you happy and relaxed and that is in turn reflected in your body: you smile, a sense of freedom brightens your heart, you breathe more freely. You wonder what's so special and you realise that first you were less observant, that you were inside yourself.

There is wonder and amazement at what you perceived, you have opened your soul to the world outside you. You have been open-minded, but that needed a special observation.

The aim of this exercise is to stimulate open-mindedness. The more knowledge and skills you have, the harder it is to be unbiased, the less you are open to new impressions. You have already made many judgments and many patterns have formed in your thinking and your actions. Imprisonment of your mind may be the result, i.e. something or someone is simply this or that and you think it will remain so forever. You're not alert to changes.

Habit determines your reaction in certain situations and to certain people. To practice open-mindedness, you must open your senses and withhold your judgments back. You want to see the world with different eyes and become full of expectation about everything around you. You try to listen to new experiences. You discover things that you did not notice before. Your attention is greater and the result is that the world is expressed in your inner self. You must not deny your already acquired knowledge,; on the contrary, you should build on and enrich it.

Helpful when practicing, is an attitude of inquiring interest and curiosity. Relish your growing amazement and wonder at the world: there are always new observations. Along with these, new questions arise.

This exercise is a combination of thinking and willing. Thinking consists of a great openness to new observations and letting events speak for themselves. Willing involves engaging everything with confidence, assuming that you can change every day and that there is always something new to be discovered.

Task: *(Chapter 5 – In your workbook)*

Take your note book or journal and write at each point when you notice something different than previously perceived in your daily events.
Ie;
You may notice while walking to the bus stop that you can smell toast being prepared.
You may notice someone's dinner being cooked as you pull up at traffic lights on the way home.
You may notice the smell of tobacco as you walk down the street amongst strangers.

You may notice that the dirtiest lawn in the street has had the grass cut !

No matter what it is ... write down your new awareness to circumstances that you may not have thought or noticed before.

This allows you to notice your awareness developing and your open-mindedness becoming stress relieving! You now notice new and different things due to your senses guiding you to new awareness, relieving you of the constant thought of worry or stress patterns.

6. Inner harmony

- creating balance

Practice the five previous exercises, separately and in various combinations as needed, so that harmony between thinking, feeling and willing arises.

The previous exercises were aimed at the separate development of soul qualities: control of thought and willing, equanimity with respect to feelings of love and sorrow, positivity in assessing the world and open-mindedness towards life.

This exercise is designed to ensure harmony between these qualities. Through practicing the five exercises together, according to need, harmony will be created between the three faculties of the soul.

You can practice combinations of exercises for a while, but you can also choose a specific exercise that you need in a certain phase in your life.

Perhaps it gets too much after a while. Then it may help to think that someone who practices, learns and grows, and someone who does not. The exercises get easier because you have practiced them separately at first; you can do them to some extent.

You have already gathered experience, acquired skills and built forces that will make it easier to continue. You've already become more attentive to your soul, you improved on your weaknesses and limitations and you already react more balanced than before. By going through this exercise you will improve this further.

After you've done all the exercises once, you can stop for a while and then start again or just do the exercises that did not go well.

In this way the basic exercises can be a help to develop yourself continually.

Chapter 4

Meditation

"Meditation is all about the
pursuit of nothingness.
It's like the ultimate rest.
It's better than the
best sleep you've ever had.
It's a quieting of the mind.
It sharpens everything, especially
your appreciation of your
surroundings.
It keeps life fresh."

Hugh Jackman

Meditation

is a part of the therapeutic process.

Meditation relates to spiritual growth and
development of the mind.

Whilst you meditate your body reduces oxygen consumption,
eliminates carbon dioxide and reduces the rate and volume of
respiration. Additionally, meditation is found to decrease blood-
lactate levels, slow your heartbeat, improves skin health, and
soothes anxiety and panic disorders.

Meditating regularly will actually give you better emotional
balance and overall well-being.

Beyond the physical benefits, it assists you to build internal
energy, promotes relaxation, and encourages compassion, love,
patience generosity and forgiveness. It also creates an altered
state of awareness, a suspension of logical thought and the
maintenance of a self-observing attitude. This is a major tool for
self-development, and will be needed to achieve enlightenment.

Researchers at the University of Massachusetts found that those
who meditated approximately half an hour per day during an
eight-week period reported that at the end of the period, they
were better able to act in a state of awareness and observation.
Respondents also said they felt non-judgmental (Harvard's
Women's Health Watch, 2011).

The report "Meditation as Medicine" (American Academy of Neurology) cites scientific evidence from various studies which claim that meditation can increase attention span, sharpen focus, improve memory, and dull the perception of pain.

So will we need to practice these techniques on a regular basis in the beginning, until you are generally more relaxed and you notice you have better concentration.

The more you practice the easier it becomes. This will require self-discipline, like all of the exercises that you undertake to achieve mindfulness, but the rewards are worth the effort.

How to meditate

ou can find meditation classes in your local area which perform guided group meditations. Some prefer to learn this way initially and then set aside time throughout their daily routine for meditating alone.

Set aside 2 times a day to be still, such the transition between night and day, day and night are ideal or when you waken and before you sleep may be easier. Start by having a stretch to loosen your muscles, allowing you to sit comfortably, upright with your legs crossed or beneath you if you are sitting in a chair, or to lie with your arms along your side palm down.

Begin breathing slowly and deeply, in through your nose and out through your mouth. This is called circular breathing. This will slow your heart rate, relax your muscles and focuses the mind. Simply concentrate on each breath as it comes into your body, slowly and exhale out allowing yourself to feel your stresses and worries expel with each breath.

You might find it easier to take a breath, slowly count 1, 2, exhale, 1, 2, inhale 1, 2 exhale 1, 2 ... this will assist taking deep breathes and holding for a moment, it will also help you to clear the mind. If you do get thoughts popping up, try to just see them flow out with each exhale and just count to clear your thoughts, then as you slowly stop counting and just feel each breath in and out.

Once your mind is clear and you are in a relaxed state, start to imagine a staircase, with 20 steps, every 5 breathes take a step down, feel the movement and just breathe.

Once you are totally relaxed and at the bottom of the staircase, you glide towards a door that leads outside, you slowly walk down the garden path towards a gate in the fence, walk through the gate a see where it leads you...

If you choose to be in a field, smell the grass, look around at the horizon, see the trees and sit quietly so you can hear all the birds ... relax and breathe

You may choose an old tree that has a huge opening, you climb into the opening to find your favorite cushion, sit and relax ... smell and listen to the surrounds.. relax and breathe

Try this relaxation meditation;

Meditation tips

You may fly...

You may see spirit angels, let your imagination take you to worlds beyond our physical realm... feel free, use your senses of smell touch, feel, hear the surrounds ... be in the place wholly with your spirit.

Meditation should last for at least 3 minutes, ideally 20-30 minutes. There are no exact rules; the main goal is to block out your thoughts, focus your mind and associate with your soul and help us detach.

Try using a candle. Meditating with eyes closed can be challenging for a beginner. Lighting a candle and using it as your point of focus allows you to strengthen your attention with a visual cue. This can be very powerful.

The core of meditation is to focus and eventually quiet your mind, freeing your awareness and achieving a state of deeper self-awareness. As you progress, you will find that you can meditate at anytime, anywhere, accessing an inner calm no matter what's going on around you. You will have better control your reactions to things as you become increasingly aware of your thoughts (letting go of anger, for example.)

Tips

- Don't meditate when you are full or hungry
- Make sure you are comfortable before you start
- Remove yourself from distraction or interruption

- Slowly come out of mediation, opening your eyes and sit for a moment longer to gather your awareness back into your physical realm.
- minutes every day is better than 20 minutes once a week
- I like to track back to the door at the beginning of the pathway (mediation), and open my eyes once I open the door, however you come back, do so peacefully.
- Use a meditation affirmation, an example can found at the end of this chapter

Common Scenarios

ome meditation exercise's for you to do:

Sit comfortably, breathe for a few minutes and relax

Imagine that you on a white sandy beach, in the early morning, surrounded by a light, hazy mist. The sun is rising slowly. You can feel the warm, morning light on your face and your body. You are content and at ease. Relaxed.

The sand beneath your bare feet is soft and warm. A light breeze caresses your face. This beach is deserted. You have it all to yourself, and you have all the time in the world. Listen to the soothing sound of the ocean. The waves are gently breaking along the shore. Begin to walk slowly through the mist towards the water. A small boat is waiting for you.

The boat is bobbing calmly in the walk, tied to the shore with a strong rope. Walk to the water's edge and step into the boat.

You are feeling completely at peace, completely safe, and completely relaxed. When you are ready, untie the rope...and let it go.

Relax, and allow the natural currents of the ocean to guide you away from the beach.
Your boat drifts smoothly. It rocks ever so gently in the water. This rocking motion relaxes you even more deeply. The sun is now higher in the sky. Its light has gathered strength.

Notice that the mist that surrounds you is beginning to evaporate. You can see the air becoming clearer and clearer. Watch as the sun's rays dissolve all of the mist. Now you can see clearly in all directions. It's as though a veil has been lifted.

Sparkling ocean water surrounds you on all sides, and in front of you, a small island comes into view. Your boat moves closer and closer to the island, gliding slowly and effortlessly through the water. The island is drenched in sunlight. It is covered in palm trees that sway gently in the breeze.

Your boat glides slowly forward, and comes to rest on the shore.

You have arrived. Step out of the boat and take a moment to appreciate this place of sublime beauty. Exotic birds dance from tree to tree, and brilliantly coloured flowers grow in abundance. The air itself seems to shimmer and vibrate with pure, luminous energy. You take in the soothing sound of the wind as it passes through the trees.

In this place, you are free from all memories of the past. You are free from all concerns about the future. You are free from all responsibilities. This is a place of total peace, and it is all yours.

You notice an opening between the palm trees. In the centre of this opening, there is a narrow path that leads deep into a rich green forest. Begin your journey into the heart of the forest. Follow the path as it meanders between columns of ancient trees. This forest seems familiar to you, like the memory of a pleasant dream, or a place you visited as a child. Walk deeper into the forest. You are guided by a force that you trust, and that makes you feel safe, nurtured and still.

You have reached the very heart of the forest. Before you is a shimmering pond of crystal clear water, perfectly still, round, and brimming with pure spring water.

Notice that the water is like a mirror, free from even the slightest ripple.
 All the trees have become motionless. As each moment passes, the world around you becomes more and more calm, and you yourself become more and more still.
Feel yourself sliding into a deep state of relaxation. In this pond, your thoughts simply melt away.

All is still and silent, the only sound is the waves in the distance.

Slowly bring your awareness back to the pond. You are deeply relaxed and refreshed. Now it's time to make your way back home. Follow the path back to your boat.
You arrive back at the entrance to the forest. Your boat is waiting for you, just where you left it. Walk to the water's edge, and climb into the boat.

You feel relaxed and secure. You know that your boat will bring you home safely. Your journey is effortless and calm. Like all of the moments in your life...effortless and calm.
Relax, and allow the current to guide you. You arrive at the beach.
Step out of the boat and onto the sand.

You are home.
Slowly become aware of the room in which you sit.
Wiggle your toes and slightly wiggle your fingers
When you are ready to... open your eyes.
Take your time and give yourself a few minutes before you get up.

Scenario 2

Sit comfortably and relax

Now close your eyes. Allow each breath to carry away all stress and tension as the air goes out of your lungs. Take another slow breath in through your nose. Fill your lungs completely. Hold it for a moment, release the breath through your mouth. Empty your lungs completely. Feel that the tension in your body has begun to loosen. Take another deep breath, hold it for a moment, and then let it go. Feel yourself relaxing more and more with each breath.

Bring your awareness to your feet and toes. Now breathe in deeply through your nose, and as you do, gradually curl your toes down and tense the muscles in the soles of your feet. Hold your breath for just a few seconds and then release the muscles in your feet as you exhale.

Now move your awareness to your calf muscles. Breathe in deeply and point your toes up towards your knees and tighten these muscles. Hold for just a moment, then let those muscles go limp as you breathe out.

Now take a deep breath in, and tense the muscles in your thighs. Hold for just a moment, then release all those muscles. Focus on letting them go limp and loose as you exhale.

Draw in a deep breath and slowly tighten the muscles in your buttocks. Hold this for a few seconds, then release. Feel the tension leaving your muscles as you breathe out.

Inhale and then tighten your stomach muscles. Hold for a moment. Now release your breath and let your muscles relax as you breathe out.

Bring your awareness to the muscles in your back. As you slowly breathe in, arch your back slightly to tighten these muscles....release your breath and let the muscles relax.

Pull your shoulders up towards your ears and squeeze these muscles as you breathe in deeply, let your muscles to go limp and loose as you breath out

Enjoy the feeling of the heaviness in your body. Breathe in and clench your fists, tighten the muscles in your arms. Squeeze the muscles as you hold your breath...now release and gently breathe all the way out. Let your arms and hands go loose and limp.

Tighten the muscles in your face by squeezing your eyes shut and clenching your lips together. Breathe in, hold for a moment...now breathe out and relax. Feel your face softening.

Take a deep breath in, and then open your mouth as wide as you can. Feel your jaw muscles stretching and tightening. Exhale and allow your mouth to gently close.

Take one final deep breath in, filling your lungs completely...hold for just a moment, then release and relax. Let all that air carry away all of your tension.

You are now completely relaxed, from the tips of your toes to the top of your head. Enjoy this feeling for as long as you like. Take your time, and when you are ready, slowly open your eyes.

Scenario 3

Imagine walking down a busy city street full of shops and businesses. You can see crowds of people hurrying from one place to another. See the cars and buses on the road. As you walk along the sidewalk, you notice a narrow doorway.... You walk towards it, and step inside the narrow entrance.

You take a few steps deeper inside and find yourself at the top of a flight of stairs.
You slowly walk down the steps, as you do the sound of the city begins to fade away. With each step you take, you feel yourself moving away from the noise of the world, and down into a place of deep quiet. As you gradually walk down the steps, you sink deeper and deeper into a state of peaceful relaxation.

When you reach the bottom of the stairs, you feel calm and deeply relaxed. You can barely hear the sound of the street above...it seems far away.
You see a tall wooden door with no handle to open it, study the door more closely and you notice that the word "release" has been carved into its surface. Contemplate this word. Feel the essence of it.

Slowly you begin to feel a sensation of opening, of letting go, of releasing, and the door unlocks, creaking as it slowly opens. You see a small room filled with bookshelves.
You step inside the room, and slowly the door closes behind you.

This room is a private place, secluded and inviting. It has no windows and it is very, very quiet. You feel content and secure in this place.

In the centre of the room sits is a wooden desk, on which sits a large, old book. You pick up the book, feeling its weight in your hands. You feel a sense of wonder as you hold this grand, old book covered in dust, and you realise it has rested in this place for a long time...waiting for you since long before you were born. You open the cover and notice that all the pages are blank.

This is a book of freedom. It has the power to free you from anything in life that might be bothering you or weighing you down.

It is time for you to write in the book. Take a moment to think about anything that is troubling you in your life. Bring to mind any situation that seems to be blocking you. Any person who you are in conflict with. Any negative feelings you are holding on to. Write about anything at all that you feel is holding you back, or that burdens you. There is no right or wrong way to do this. Simply feel or imagine your thoughts and feelings being imprinted into this book. Take your time. Allow images to form in your mind, and allow your feelings to flow. Let them flow out onto the pages of the book.

Sense that the pages are filling up with all your worldly concerns. The book absorbs them all. As the pages fill with words and pictures, you begin to feel lighter and more positive. You have been heard. You have been understood. You feel reassured and relieved.

When you are ready you close the book, you watch in amazement as the domed roof above you begins to open. Slowly but surely, the roof opens completely, revealing the clear blue sky above. You stand with your arms by your side, observing the sky.

You gently raise your forearms and hands, your palms facing away from you, and as you do, your body begins to float, and your feet lift off the floor. A wave of exhilaration flows through you as you realize that you have the freedom to fly anywhere you choose. As you raise your hands, you float higher. When you lower them, you gently descend.
With effortless ease, you begin to float towards the open roof above you. You glide up and out of the room and slowly up into the sky.

You feel a wonderful sense of freedom as you fly higher and higher in the sky. You can see the entire city below which is gradually becoming smaller and smaller. You are leaving the world behind and floating high up into the heavens.

Higher and higher you fly, passing beyond the clouds, feeling even more joyful, even more free. Now, you decide to fly right out into the cosmos, leaving all of your concerns far behind you. With your arms raised, you ascend higher and higher, travelling beyond the skies and out into space.

You turn to look back on the Earth. It is a small blue sphere, floating in emptiness.
Admire the beauty of the stars and the planet far below as you drift, weightless and at peace.

This floating sensation is relaxing and you slip even deeper into a state of complete stillness. You feel as though you are a million miles from anything or anyone, and yet, you feel connected to the entire universe. You feel weightless.

From deep within the silent space inside you, a voice can be heard.

Its loving words echo in your mind...

(Use the meditation affirmation found on the next page)

Meditation Affirmation

I am without beginning or ending. I am eternal.
I am free to experience life in any way I choose.
My consciousness is not bound by time or space.
Like the universe itself, I am limitless.
I am a part of a vast, unified wholeness.

I am free from all concerns about the past.
I am free from all concerns about the future.
My life is in perfect order, and it unfolds according to a perfect plan.

I do not strive to attain the things that I desire;

I simply allow them to flow to me.
I release my grip on life.
I am calm in the knowledge that all my needs are taken care of.

I am open to all of life's experiences.
As the moments of my life come and go, I am at peace.
I do not judge these moments. I welcome them. I observe them.
I accept them all.

If problems arise, I do not resist them.

I observe them with a calm, open mind, for I know that they will resolve in time...

I yearn for nothing, I am in harmony with the universe

Meditation tasks

Task 1
Write out a peaceful meditation for yourself.
*Write about a place you would love to visit, the things it may
have and the experiences you would like. I know of people who
go to heavenly places and see cherubs and angels and fly with
them.*

There is no limit to where or what you can do.

Task 2   (Chapter 6 – In your workbook)

Write out a meditation affirmation.
*Affirming all of the beliefs of the universe, allowing yourself to be
consumed with the powers at large and surrender to being one
with the universe.*

*You will learn how to write affirmations in Chapter 6, the more
affirmations you write the easier it will be for you to recollect
them as you meditate.*

Find the audio for each scenario here;

Meditation is the dissolution of thoughts in Eternal awareness or Pure consciousness without objectification, knowing without thinking, merging finitude in infinity.

- Voltaire

Chapter 5

Goal Setting

"Setting goals
is the first step in
turning the invisible
into the visible."

Tony Robbins

Setting goals

Goal setting gives you long term vision and short term motivation. By setting clearly defined goals, you can measure and take pride as you achieve and progress.

As you achieve goals you have set, your confidence will rise and you will feel more in control of your life and its direction. This will also strengthen your motivation as you recognise your own ability and competence.

You need to have a vision of where you would like to be in 1 year, 5 years, 10 years, 20 years… To do this, you must realise what it is you want to achieve or where you would like your life to be.
Writing down goals sets them in motion and sets a foundation in your subconscious mind by giving a detailed set of instructions to work on. The more precise your goals are, the more efficient your subconscious mind can become.

Shoot for the moon… because if you miss you will still land amongst the stars! Make sure your goal is high enough; the universe will work out the "how". Know what you want and what you would like to achieve in your life

Task: *(Chapter 7 – In your workbook)*
In your workbook, write out your short term and long term goals. Set goals for this month, this year, 2 years, 5 years, 10 years and 20 years.
Write down everything you would like to achieve during the rest of your life.

One of the best ways is to imagine your life to be limitless... get a cork board and each time you see something in a magazine or newspaper that you like, cut it out and pin it to the board. This is called a vision board. Find a picture of your dream home, the lounge suite you would love to be sitting on, the car you want to drive, how much money you would like to have, the camera or watch or whatever it is you would like to have in your life and

Vision board

Your vision board is your ultimate manifestation of what you desire, or in other words, action boards for achieving. Also known as dream boards, vision boards are how you would like to be living, affirming what you would like and what makes you happy, it also helps you stay motivated for positive change.

It will become your inspiring place, where you sit for a moment each day, look to the pictures and close your eyes and feel as if you have them already.

Feel how your life would be, imagine that you are among them now. You can divide the items into categories: Achievements, Spirituality, Work, Wealth, Family, Finances, and Relationships.

Drawing your own pictures for your vision board will help the visions or desires to resonate with your subconscious more, use colour in the pictures which help trigger more realisation to your subconscious mind.

Everything that you put or draw onto your vision board must be positive.

You need to make the board very "visual", your subconscious mind works in pictures and images, so use as many pictures as you can. You can cut out words or phrases but make sure they resonate with you emotionally.

 The mere sight of your vision board needs to create a positive emotional response from you every time you look at it; it is there to fuel your passion.

Gazing each day at the powerful images you assemble on the board will amplify the mind's frequencies out to the universe and assist in attracting them faster as you put more feeling and passion when drawing it.

Task

Get a cork board and a few magazines that interest you. Or a sketch pad & some colour pencils. Go through the magazines, draw or cut out all of the things that resonate within you, that you would like to do or have... Now stick them all to the cork board in a visually appealing way.

(You can use a vision book, but it is best to have a board as you can place it in a predominate spot that you will see everyday.)

How to use your vision board

Place it in a strategic place for maximum exposure, like above your mirror in your bedroom, stuck to the ceiling above your bed so you can look at it every time you wake up or go to sleep, or at the back of your pantry if you use it often enough. Make sure it is somewhere that you will see it often.

Make sure that it is out of other people's sight if you are sensitive to what other say about your dreams. Their criticism or negative thoughts can damage the energy or increase your self-doubt. Keep if safe from prying eyes if needed!

It is very important that you see your vision board regularly and take a moment to contemplate having all the things now, for this you need to close your eyes and be in that picture: walk around your new home, look at the time on that watch you want, feel yourself driving the car of your dreams, you must visualise yourself after these events have occurred or as if they are in your possession.

When you focus on your vision board with intent, you will get progressively closer to achieving it. You are confirming your order with the universe, which will automatically create necessary scenarios or experiences to ensure you take the right actions to make your goals a reality.

The results are so quick you won't believe it, and you will start to experience higher levels of joy and happiness almost immediately, finding yourself on the cusp of an exhilarating change as you discover the amazing internal power to control every situation in your life.

Task

Put your board in a predominant location and make the time to look at your board daily.

Take at least 2 minutes every day to focus on its content, imagine you are at the location or with the object, how it feels, the joy you have from achieving having it in your life.

Daydream

Day dreaming is a short term detachment from your immediate surroundings. Your contact with reality becomes blurred as your mind melds into whatever you are day-dreaming about.

It is where fantasy and imagination rule, filled with happy thoughts, hopes and ambitions. Day dreaming is a part of wish-fulfillment.

Day dreaming brings several health benefits: relaxation, lowers blood pressure, relieves boredom, improves memory, curbs anxiety, promotes an active and well-equips the brain. It can also boost productivity, improve clarity of thought, and will cement your beliefs and values, creating a sense of knowing yourself and what you stand for.

Daydream when you are on the bus, or waiting around for something/someone or any doing an activity where you can take a moment to daydream about what you desire. If you are starting to feel frustrated, annoyed or bored, take the time to tune out and escape, daydream about what life has ahead. Its most important benefit is that it boosts your mood, anytime, anywhere.

So take time whenever you can to daydream for a moment and put yourself where you desire to be....!

Task   *(Chapter 7 – In your workbook)*

Write down a few daydreams to help you get started.
Imagine what you want, or where you would love to be.

Make sure you take the time at least 5 times per day to start,
until you have created a habit of daydreaming when you can find
time.

The S.M.A.R.T method

The secret to your success is determined by your goals and daily agenda. Plan to grow both consciously and subconsciously. Having your vision board is giving your subconscious mind direction, allowing your desires to be acknowledged.

The purpose for goal setting is to break down the end result into smaller stepping stones to get you to the desired result. Therefore goals need to maintained as you progress, as each "step" takes you closer to your goal new steps may become apparent or required steps now clearer, so continually updating the progress and reevaluating the highest priority "steps" first.

Goals are a form of motivation that sets the standard for self-satisfaction with performance. Achieving the goal one has set for oneself is a measure of success, and being able to meet job challenges is a way one measures success in the workplace.

Earl Nightingale said "if a person will spend one hour a day on the same subject for five years, that person will be an expert of that subject"

Wikipedia explains goal setting;

Goal setting involves establishing *specific, measurable, achievable, realistic and time-targeted* (S.M.A.R.T) goals.

Work on the theory of goal-setting suggests that an effective tool for making progress is to ensure that participants in a group with a common goal are clearly aware of what is expected from them. On a personal level, setting goals helps people work towards their own objectives. Goal setting features as a major component of personal development literature.

It is considered an "open" theory, so as new discoveries are made it is modified. Studies have shown that specific and ambitious goals lead to a higher level of performance than easy or general goals.

As long as the individual accepts the goal, has the ability to attain it, and does not have conflicting goals, there is a positive linear relationship between goal difficulty and task performance.

When you set your goals, use the S.M.A.R.T method below to allow you to set the "concrete" for the goal.

Go through the list and make sure that you have detailed the process.

The S.M.A.R.T. Method will assist with goal setting.

S = Specific.   Details, details, details! Details are everything to goal setting. If you are looking to get a new car, know the make and model, the price, the exterior and interior color. Leather or cloth seats? Sporty? Two or four-door? Sunroof?

M = Measurable.

How much, how many, how will you know when you have achieved your goal? It must be measurable in quantity or quality.

A = Attainable.

You want your goal to be attainable, but still high enough that it inspires you and is worth working for. (If not, you would already have it in your possession.)

R = Relevant.

It be relevant to you. Do you believe you can achieve it? You might not know "how" you will achieve it, but you know you can achieve it.

T = Timely.

Put a date on it! When you put a date on your goal, the goal has an ending point. What happens if you don't achieve your goal by the date? Look again at your goal and decide if you still feel passionate about it, if you do, change the date if not change or improve the goal

Once you have used the S.M.A.R.T method to set your goal, break the goal down into portions. Each portion will compound together resulting in the goal being achieved.

So write out each step you will need to take to achieve that goal. Break the steps down, to baby steps, each baby steps will work towards getting the step complete, then set about each day working on your baby steps, conscious effort towards your desired result over time will result in the goal being achieved, it's that simple.

Bucket list

Your bucket list – or –
"the top 100 things I would like to do/ have before I die!"

Try to review, add-to, envision and/or take inspired action upon anything on this list.

This is simply a list numbered, from 1 - 100 of:
What I want to do:
What I want to be:
What I want to have.

For example
1 - learn an instrument
2 - find a great personal assistant
3 - take a holiday in the Bahamas
4 - be more loving with my children
5 - be more persistent with my emotional freedom techniques (EFT's)
6 - be more organized and grateful
7 – a new / renovated kitchen
8 - a law of attraction coach
9 - a fun circle of friends that inspire, motivate and entertain me.

Simply have an ongoing list of 100 things! Try to keep it all on one page, so that you know exactly what to visualise during the day dreaming moments or manifest by getting a picture of them for your vision board.

This is also a form of goal setting that provides a concrete list of things on which, when you are on your death bed at 112 years of age, you will look back and feel accomplished that you have achieved. Writing out this list affirms to your subconscious precisely what you want in life.

Task   (Chapter 7 – In your workbook)

Most importantly, get started!

This list could change and develop as you get older, you may not want to go on the fastest roller coaster later on in life, nor would you want to travel around the country in a campervan in your twenties.. so get started on your list and let it continually grow as your desires change, if you get past 100 keep going...

You are never too old

to set another goal

or

to dream

a new dream.

-C. S. Lewis

Chapter 6

Affirmations

"Practice rather than preach.

Make of your life an affirmation,

defined by your ideals,

not the negation of others.

Dare to the level of your
capability then

go beyond to a higher level."

- Alexander Haig

ffirmations

An affirmation is to declare something that is true. You are affirming your knowledge about yourself. They are used for you to know that you are special, you are more than enough, and you are smart, intelligent, and capable of anything.

When using an affirmation you must get the feeling of the affirmation for it to really have an effect. Our feeling memory is important to get through the inertia we have about encoding positives. That inertia controls the amount of resistance we have to change. You must get in the feeling of the affirmation to condition the mind.

Using positive affirmations, you can manifest change in your life. There are 1000's of affirmations, cards, sayings and quotes. They contribute to our wellbeing in tangible ways. They are self-talk or self-scripts if you like, a declaration of positive statements about yourself that condition the subconscious mind.

Although they can be positive or negative statements, surprisingly we say them to ourselves almost unknowingly: "you can't do that" or "I know I can do that" whichever you think... it is true.

Being mindful of what affirmations we say to ourselves is the first step in manifesting change. They are a powerful way to create change, used correctly they will help you achieve goals in your career, love, wealth, health, any area of your life.

They must be dedicated belief; you must believe in your unlimited potential, if you don't believe then they will be of no value to you. By the power of your thoughts, feeling the affirmation makes them believable which begins with understanding you have the power to create what you want and to become who you want to be by simply affirming who you already are and what you are capable of.

Affirmations are the key part of applying the law of attraction correctly. Wording your own affirmations, by the power of thought, you will ensure your desires are realised. They reinforce your beliefs in yourself, through feeling the affirmations your conscious mind and unconscious mind will accept these affirmations because there is no disparity between what is and what can be... then they will work.

Daily Affirmation cards are available in the Square Root of Life range,

Scan here: to get a 78 deck of "Daily Affirmation" cards

Creating your own affirmations

Always create your affirmation in the present tense; to talk about future tense is to relegate it to another day, meaning your desire is always waiting to happen. Place yourself in the situation you are wanting: i.e. "I am strong enough to tackle life's tests." Although you may essentially be talking about the future, you are placing yourself in the "now", reinforcing the belief that you truly are strong enough in the present moment – not tomorrow, not some distant point in the future, but now.

Know your strengths, and acknowledge and celebrate the character traits that you possess. Affirmations bring out the best in you, helping you create the energy to turn your dreams into a reality. "I am a good person with the ability to help others" "I am feeling great, I see myself getting better every day, in every way" "I have an endless supply of creativity, energy and tolerance"

Write affirmations as you continue to grow, be specific to what you want: habit change, attitude building, motivational or situational. They can be as plain or colourful as you like, but they should have both emotional (feeling) and cognitive (thinking) force.

Your affirmation should begin with "I am……" or "my ……." "I feel….."" "I love" "I have…" "I Know…"

It should contain: (a) Personal reference to you… (b) The present tense… (c) Emotion… and (d) Your ideal results… Such as "I (personal) am currently (present) enjoying (emotional) getting fit and becoming more healthy (result)

There is no need to rush your affirmations when creating them, you need to take time to write them for the result you desire, and that way you supercharge your frequency to the universe.

Writing about what you expect to happen, helps to dissolve any underlying doubts you may have about your affirmations and it is a powerful technique for writing affirmations.

Task: *(Chapter 8 – In your workbook)*

Practice by writing 20 affirmations, then in your journal write a new one each week

When to use affirmations

Write your affirmation a hundred times, until it has imprinted itself into your subconscious mind.

Our minds are more open to absorbing behavior change patterns when completely relaxed, some people are more relaxed first thing in the morning or last thing at night, so whatever time you find that you are more relaxed repeat the affirmations over and over in your mind, try to repeat them to yourself while you train at the gym or perform a mundane task, where you are not required to think and self-talk won't distract your train of thought.

Starting with brief affirmations of your self-perception such as:
I am a great friend..   I am a great mother..   I am a very caring person..   I am a divine being..   I am an excellent lover/partner..   I am very loving...   I am a wonderful cook..
I am a positive person...   I am powerful
These are confirming the thing you already know about yourself 100%

Then start with some affirmations that establish your ability:
I create my own universe..   I create strong bonds with people...   I create love all around me...
I created wonderful children/relationships...

Next, incorporate some gratitude affirmations about what you already have:
I have a great partner ....   I have a cozy home....
I have a unique soul....   I have a great job....
I have beautiful natured pets..

Then start to create affirmations to manifest what you want:

I have a magnificent body....   I have enough money for all that I need...
I have great health and I am indestructible...
I am conquering my illness; I am defeating it steadily each day.
My thoughts are full of positivity and my life is plentiful with prosperity ...
I wake up today with strength in my heart and clarity in my mind.

Helpful and well known affirmations

- I am loving, open and free
- I love and approve myself
- I am always in happy circumstance, happy thoughts come naturally
- I trust myself and know I make the right choices
- I only live in the present, the past is gone
- I am a unique child of the universe
- I radiate love and my heart is always open
- I matter and what I have to offer matters

- The more I love, the more love surrounds me
- I make the right choices every time
- The universe truly supports me, I am never alone
- I attract prosperity and abundance
- I know my situation will work out for the highest good
- I am my own self, I am happier now than ever
- I choose to find helpful and optimistic way to look at everything
- Connecting with others come naturally
- I know my inner self will guide me to the right decision
- I see me friends and family as gifts
- I take time to show those around me that I love them
- I have enough energy within to light up a city for a week
- I am smart and beautiful and that's how everyone sees me
- I engage in things that impacts the world in a positive way
- My thoughts are my reality, I embrace my new life
- I fill this day with hope and face it with joy
- I follow my dreams no matter what
- I have the ability and intelligence to get through anything
- I am good enough and get better everyday
- The past has no power or hold over me
- I am deeply happy with who I am

- Any thought that is passed on to the subconscious often enough and convincingly enough is finally accepted.- *Robert Collier*

- I figured that if I said it enough, I would convince the world that I really was the greatest.- *Muhammad Ali*

- It's the repetition of affirmations that leads to belief. And once that belief becomes a deep conviction, things begin to happen.- *Claude M. Bristol*

- As a man thinketh in his heart, so is he.- *Proverbs 23:7*

- Your imagination is your preview of life's coming attractions.- *Albert Einstein*

- The difference between success and mediocrity is all in the way you think.- *Dean Francis*

- As long as you know what it is you desire, then by simply affirming that it is yours -- firmly and positively, with no ifs, buts, or maybes -- over and over again- *Scott Reed*

- What we continually think about eventually will manifest in our lives. - *Sidney Madwed*

- You must begin to think of yourself as becoming the person you want to be.- *David Viscott*

- Believing there is a solution paves the way to a solution.- *Dr. David Schwartz*

- Whatever the mind of man can conceive and believe, it can achieve.- *Napoleon Hill*

- You've got to win in your mind before you win in your life.- *John Addison*
    - You can do it if you believe you can.- *Napoleon Hill*

Success is a process,

a quality of mind

and way of being,

an outgoing affirmation of life.

- Alex Noble

Action steps

Make what you do today count for tomorrow.
Make today count !

To make your growth effective, intentional and strategic you need to think it through and plan well. The more detailed you are the faster the process will create your desires. If you desire change a little everyday will make the process over the long haul.

Make the most important decisions then manage those decisions, one at a time, make every decision with the end result in mind and actively work on the little steps everyday.

To use this book in its intention, it's highly recommended that your FREE get a copy of "The Square Root of Life – Workbook"> mentioned in the Introduction.

This will enable you to go through each task in very detailed and meticulous way. It is a PDF, so you will be able to continually print off the workbook and use it over and over again; clarifying your intention.

To be able to embed these techniques in your mind, you are required to follow the tasks multiple times. Once you have mastered your mind and are able to think positive thoughts consistently you are ready to move onto the next book in this Square Root of life series; "Manifest the Ultimate Life" available & published Jan 2014.

The "Manifest the Ultimate Life" edition, goes onto detail more techniques and activities required for you to be able to take the next step in fulfilling your desire to live a better life.

Giving you the tools to turn your desires into your reality and live the life you have dreamed of.

It covers:
- Being a magnetic force
- Transmitting frequency
- Attracting and Manifesting
- Appreciation and Gratitude
- Daily and Lifetime intention
- Be enlightened

Get your copy >

You can do it
if
you believe you can.

- Napoleon Hill

ABOUT THE AUTHOR

On the 9th September 2012, my husband, life partner, father of
our 14mth old son walked out unbeknown to me – permanently.
I had a mortgage, 54k dollars in credit card debt (thanks to his
business endeavors & his new vehicle), a 14m old son to
support, 2 Rottweiler's, a half renovated home with a quickly
mounting pile of bills and no form of income.
He hadn't taken any of his belongings, not his clothes or even his
toothbrush!
Over a 3 month period my life somersaulted.
As my life dissolved in front of me, the realisation that I was
unable to support my son and was about to loose everything I
had built up over the past 12 years was very imminent.
On the edge of a nervous breakdown and having uncontrollable
bouts of hysteria and crying I could not believe the position I was
in, I broke down hourly. My doctor put me on strong anti
depressants to help ease my anguish, but they barely worked.
With hope in my heart I arranged to spend Christmas day as a
family, he was going to come sometime during the night, so he
would be there for our son when he woke up. Promising to give
some money to enable me to buy Christmas lunch prior, I used
the small amount of money I had to buy him and my son some
Christmas presents and waited for him to bring our Christmas
lunch money, an arrangement that never happened.
We woke Christmas morning, with no sign of him. I stalled in bed
with my son until 9.30, waiting for him to show- surely he would
do this to his own son on Christmas day! I walked out and tried
my best to make what was left of Christmas morning fun and
exciting for my son as he opened his presents. We received a call

at 10.50 am that he had just woken up, that he was sorry he slept in and is on his way, a 20 minute drive.

2.15pm a car pulled up out the front, he jumped out, grabbed a 6 pack of beers from the esky in the back and walked into the house, no food, no presents just his beloved beer!!

I was not impressed, he sat down barely saying anything to me opened his presents that his son gave him and it' started.

We went for a drive to find food, as he had brought money, and the comments continued, I looked at my son in the rear view mirror, looking up at me scared, knowing that his father was taunting for an argument and I asked myself how I can put my son through this again– I kicked him out of the car about 8 minutes into the drive.

We went home and ate 2 minute noodles for Christmas lunch and pasta for dinner, I swore that would be the first and last horrible Christmas my son would ever have to endure, and set about to change my situation.

==============================

My name is Sarah Davis and I have written these books to empower you to take control of your life, and live however you truly desire, as I now do. It is a hard struggle to become happy in times of severe distress and these are the techniques that helped me leave my past behind me, move on and recreate myself.

After learning so much about life and how I can orchestrate the events and experiences I encounter, I wanted to share this knowledge so others can learn an easy path to achieving their goals.

I am now a Certified Law of Attraction Advanced Practitioner thanks to Global sciences foundation, my life has completely flipped around, as I intended. I have also completed my NLP Advanced Practitioner certification, Reiki Masters and Hypnosis communicator training.

My intention now is to teach others who may be struggling or going through some trail in their life, "how" to arrange, coordinate, and manipulate the elements in order to achieve their goals, giving them total control of their destiny.

Many readers searching for ways to use the Law of Attraction fail, as I did initially, because of failing to remove a lifetime worth of struggles resulting in mental ailments, this impedes success when using this powerful law.

This book series is written for them especially.

I hope that this book series shows you the power to create whatever life you would like, as it has for me.

Action steps and formulating a process for others to follow is the only way I know to teach others how to achieve life changing intentional redirection, by sharing the techniques that worked for me.

====================================

"Manifest The Ultimate Life" is the second book in this series, out January 2014. If you would like to be notified when it is available, please feel free to email me at; tosarahdavis@gmail.com or like the *Square Root of Life* - FB page

Opt in to win a hard cover copy of this book- 5 to be won; http://squarerootoflife.com.au/

You will not receive any form of marketing or spam unrelated to the publication of books in this series, I will never give or sell your information to anyone else. This is my personal email address; personal messages are welcome and enjoyed, spam or marketing not appreciated or tolerated.

You can also like my facebook pages "Law of attraction coach Sydney" or "Success at home" for some inspiration

Thank you.

Sarah

If you would like one on one coaching please contact +61 422 648 079

NB; Scan this for: Manifest the Ultimate Life Happiness Kits, Energy Bracelets, Inspirational Quote cards & audio content.

Or go to www.squarerootoflife.com.au/shop

Thank you ☺ Sarah

I hope you like the products & series.

"There are risks and costs to action.

But they are far less

than the long range risks of

comfortable inaction."

John F. Kennedy

Acknowledgements

Mr Michael Kirton BA, MA (hons) Psych (Cant), G.Th, ASSD (Melb) MAPS.

Whose expertise, understanding and patience lead me to become the person I am today. His unbelievable skills and knowledge in all areas of the human psyche gave me the ability to relieve psychological distress and promote wellbeing through personal development. And he taught me many of the tools I have shared with you in this book.
He has the strongest mind, kindest heart and has been my biggest influence.
"You empowered me to take control of my mind and my life;
I am forever in your debt. Thank you"

The Law of Attraction teachers
Appreciation and gratitude to the team who created "The Secret", as a movie. I read "The Power" a year before I was introduced to The Secret, but it didn't resonate like when I watched the movie a few years ago, many many times! Thus starting my infatuation with the Law of Attraction, the philosophy behind our connection with the universe, and the magnetic power our minds are truly capable of. The Teachings of Abraham, Conversations with God, & many more.

My mother
Who raised me with unconditional love, brought us from unbelievable hardship to a new country which she described it as "the land of opportunity". Who continually strived and struggled through all kinds of calamity to single handedly provided everything we needed, while teaching us that commitment, hard work and persistence pays off every time.

"Thank you for being such a strong woman and an amazing mother."

Most Helpful Customer Reviews
5.0 out of 5 stars **Excellently empowering** December 28, 2013
By Meghan TOP 500 REVIEWER -
I have seen quite a number of supposedly life-changing books about positive thinking, but Sarah Davis' 'Positive thinking for Life' is perhaps THE ONLY book that strikes the issue at its heart. For starters, Sarah succeeds in fleshing out thoroughly the whys and how's of how to make positive thinking a permanent part of our lives.

The key word there is "unintended", as Sarah so brilliantly elucidates in her book. 'Positive thinking for Life', in essence, is about giving us back the power over our own thoughts, actions, and eventually, our life. The book teaches us how to stop those negative things, however "unintended" they may be, and thereby empowering us like never before. A solid five-star rating for this one.

5.0 out of 5 stars
Enlightening guide to a better life December 28, 2013
By C -
This book is one of the most helpful books in getting your life where you want it to be that I've read. What makes the book so inspirational and helpful is that the author actually explains situations or things the reader has to do.
Very inspirational, educational, and teaches the reader perseverance through hard times and beginning again when things don't go as planned. It was very easy to understand and follow as well, which makes it even more useful.

5.0 out of 5 stars

Will inspire you and give you the tools at the same time December 24, 2013 By V Marra

This book pulls together elements of NLP, the Secret, Tony Robbins, yogic teachings, mind mapping, and more, with the goal of inspiring you and teaching you how to reach your goals and live the life you deserve.

What I liked about it is that, it also gives you a lot of practical tools and techniques that you can start applying in your life today to make progress toward fulfilling your goals, living your best life, and being the best you.

5.0 out of 5 stars **A blessing** December 31, 2013

By Ggreen

A classic case of a great book, as the author lets it all out, and leaves me feeling way better about myself as other readers will agree. The art of positive thinking has always been somewhat of a mysterious thing (well for me that is) now thanks to this perfect book my understanding of it all explains why I felt the way I did before I read this book, now it all makes sense. I must recommend this book to everyone who yearns for a good life changing read.

5.0 out of 5 stars **No Where Else Will You Find This Type of Actionable Information** December 31, 2013

By alb8475

The first thing that stands out to me about this book is that Sarah gives you the tools to change your mental state. I have read several books on the power of positive thinking for work and this one by far is the best that I have read. She does not just explain what it is, but she sets you up with tools to put it into action in your own life.

Excellent book and excellent resources.

√Life

THE SQUARE ROOT OF LIFE

It only takes one

One cell to create a living thing

One dream to create a life

One hope to return life from hopelessness

One person to save a life

One tree to sprout a thousand vines

One thought to become a reality

One book to change your thoughts

One idea to change your mindset

If you had to come up with the number of total life experiences you have encountered until today, it would be the tens of thousands. We lead a complex existence that has endless experiences. These seemingly unrelated experiences make up who we are today, they define how we think, how we respond and react to the world around us.

The square root of life = YOU

SARAH DAVIS

the SQUARE
ROOT
of LIFE

√Life

MANIFEST THE ULTIMATE LIFE

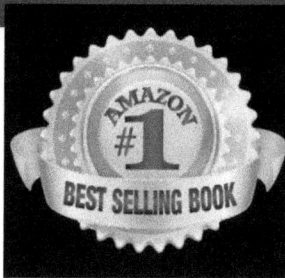

AMAZON
#1
BEST SELLING BOOK

1 on 1

Personalised Mentoring

Individual one on one coaching available from the author; Sarah Davis. For individuals who want to improve their results in any and all areas of their life. Everyone is different so sessions are tailored for you specifically based on a proven structure.

Make a committment to yourself, and allow me to guide you through stages to achieve your desires both personally & in business. Sessions are recommended weekly or fortnightly for the best results. I work with adults of all ages including troubled youths, mentoring programs, women entrepreneurs, small business coaching and enlightenment.

- Initial free consultation - an overview of where you're at now, and where you want to be
- One-on-one coaching sessions. Approximately 1 hour each
- Email support
- Phone support - for those moments when you just need to talk to someone for some support and encouragement
- Tools and resources to ensure you can keep yourself on track between coaching sessions and after the coaching process has completed

Areas of Focus

There are 6 main areas that are focused on with clients:

*	Business/Career	*	Finances
*	Relationships	*	Health & Fitness
*	Emotional State	*	Spirituality

If coaching sounds like it might be for you, take the next step and contact me today. You have absolutely nothing to lose and everything to gain by making a call or sending an email. Never be afraid of asking for help.

I have the know-how, knowledge & expertise to excel you in any area that you wish to enhance.

Contact me direct to discuss rates & options.

Sarah Davis
+61 422 648 079

tosarahdavis@gmail.com

2 x #1 Amazon Best Selling Author - Square Root of Life series

V.A & L.C > Virtual assistant & Life coach certifications

T.M & S.M.M.B > Time management, Social Media Marketing for Business certs.

Cert. NLP Advanced, Practitioner (masters)

Cert. Hypnosis Communicator - Basic & Advanced

2 x #1 Amazon Best Selling Author – (Tales 4 Tots)

Best Seller Impact training - Digital authors' academy

Cert. Law of Attraction Basic & Advanced Practitioner

Bachelor of education – EC – Curtin University

Cert IV Business Management